Kerouac In Spirit: Book II

Richard Wlodarski

ISBN: 978-93-6354-272-3

First Edition: 2024
Rs. 200/-

Cyberwit.net
HIG 45 Kaushambi Kunj, Kalindipuram
Allahabad - 211011 (U.P.) India
http://www.cyberwit.net
Tel: +(91) 9415091004
E-mail: info@cyberwit.net

Printed at Repro India Limited.

Dedicated to the memory and spirit of Adam Purcelewski.

Introduction

The spirit of Kerouac is haunting me. Not the kind of haunting that has seized your mind and body after a loved one has died. Not the kind of haunting that creates insomnia after acknowledging a life of regret. Nor any other haunting that one might possibly conceive.

The haunting spirit of Kerouac is a positive energy that has infused my mind and body with an abundance of creativity. It is there throughout the night in both my dreams and nightmares. In dreams, his spirit takes me on wondrous journeys suffused with love and peace. Unconditional Love and Peace yet to be experienced! In nightmares, his spirit guides me in overcoming fear. It's there pushing me off a mountain cliff...instructing me to fly like an eagle. It's there when I'm drowning...filling my lungs with air to safely surface. His spirit is there when The Grim Reaper is knocking on my door...telling me not to answer...I still have other doors to open.

Kerouac's spirit has taken on a life of its own. It permeates this compelling collection of poetry that captures the essence of Jack Kerouac's spirit through a modern lens. Deftly blending spirituality with contemporary events, it has created a tapestry of verses that are both starkly disturbing, yet surprisingly optimistic. The poems delve into the spiritual journey, reflecting on the quest for higher understanding and enlightenment.

Throughout this book and the continuing books in my magnum opus, **The Kerouac Venture**, I address Kerouac's personal loss and the healing process. His novels, poetry, music and meditation were the mediums he valued to work through his grief. My poems are the vehicle that his spirit works through to enhance that grief, enabling the reader to have that much more empathy. Thus, offering solace and hope to readers experiencing similar emotions.

This book, and the others in the evolving series, juxtapose the chaotic nature of Kerouac's life with moments of deep introspection. They examine how moments in his life, and indeed contemporary events, impact our consciousness and spiritual well-being.

Kerouac In Spirit: Book II and the entire **The Kerouac Venture** are noted for a cohesive blend of thought and style, creating a seamless flow that mirrors a communion of life experiences and spiritual insights. They are a rich and multifaceted read appealing to those interested in Kerouac's spirituality, personal growth and the human condition.

Richard Wlodarski

Contents

Aces For Jack

Time to call
The damn bluff
Poker-faced
Aces for Jack

Aged Youth

When I was young
Misunderstood
In such damn times
I walked aged
In such wisdom

All Talent

No such thing
As lack of
Damn talent

Brain ain't dormant
Thrives on yours/mine
Creative source
Allen Ginsberg's Secret

Sleep all day long
Miss morning light
Such sun's delight
For what I long

Wolf's howling tonight
Ginsberg so damn bright
Whispers to me in delight
Secret's secret such damn fright
And...I'm on the road again

Allen Ginsberg's Secret

Did his friends
See his art
Before him?
After him?
Or with him?

Atonement

Woke up mornin'
Distastin' night
Brain's a stirrin'
For some groovin'
Music to likin'
Playin' in background
Of my last damn sound
Mind in the foreground
Tastes sins of the past
Cries for forgiveness

Barfly

Bullshit, friend
Your days are
Damn numbered
In numbed bars

Beat's Curse

You screwed me
On such night
Every night...
I forgive you

Birth Of Sin

Christ died
For me
Yet, sin's
My name

Bittersweet Life
I'm brandied
For candy
Just watch me

Black Clouds Dispersing

I don't taste
This damn life
When I wake
To black clouds
When life's bitch
Has cursed me
Bleak day there
Not here

I so wake
In respect
To Good Life
And I thank God

Black Dog's Visitation

On such nights
When I'm death
Angels come
Devils fly

I'm alive

Bluesy Talk

Talkin' to you
Through words of blue
Do you even
Damn understand?

Born In France

To taste croissant
In home of France
Baguette to go
With wine and cheese
To rise above
Eiffel Tower
And be so pleased
Nothing to sneeze
About in land
Of romantic
Squeeze in the please

Broke Not Busted

Busted
No dough
For show
Forego
Damn fame?
No goddam
Shaming way

By The Grace Of Candlelight

I write in blackness
Of such lonely night
Searching ray of light
Blindness prevails
Yet... eyes search for soul

Cleverly Foolish

Sometimes
Such a
Damn ass
Other
Time now
Human
Boring
Always
Alert

Cloak And Dagger

Secret agent man
Maybe your neighbour
Maybe your best friend
Maybe God's disguise

Darkness

Candlelight
So lost now
Like my soul

Death Of The Word

Screw them
Bastards
Who killed
The damned
Sacred word

Death The Adventure

Death's not the end
Just beginning
Of adventure
Yet so unknown

Done!

Job's done now
So complete
Fait complit

Door Mat

Don't treat me
Like damn shit
When you're pissed

Dr. Sax The Shadow

The shadow
Doesn't need
The damned light
Follows me
Everywhere

Dulling The Mind

What's the point
Of dullness
Of sharp mind

Emotions Prevail

Couldn't think
Of that much
To now say
So I cried
When you died

Entity

You are sure
You're damn dead? ...
'cause I'm still
Writing now
...And that's you!

Exhaustion

I'm not
Alive
'til I'm
So dead

Fake It Forward

Yesterday was
Just tomorrow
In dark disguise

Fed Up

I'm dead tired
Of such crap
Makes my head
Rewired

Feeling Death

Tragic desolate soul
Traversing universe
Guided by The Spirit...
Out of my goddamn mind

Brandy is fine
Uppers quicker
Good talk with Ginsberg
Softens the all else

New York's not my home
Wolfe would have howled
At stark raving moon
I feel his death

Finally Free

Good night, my friend
Life has been kind
To you and me
Thank God we're free

Forgive Damn Fool

How I so suffered
Through the damn blindness
In both you and me

How I so cried
In mid of night
'til morning light

How I so fried
Out of my life
Morning's desire

Forgive this damn fool

Forward Ending

The end
Begins
When life's
At end

Free Mind

I ain’t no saint
Don’t circumvent
Bastardly vent

Gerard Calling

Stay close to me
I'm almost dead
Now than later
You make me better

I feel Heaven now
Gerard is calling me
I'm still so goddamn scared
The White Dove sits there...stared

Getting An Ulcer...Just For You

I'll cry when
I do feel
The need for it
Now I'll sit
On this damn pain
Absorb the crap
Get an ulcer
Blame it on you

Getting To Know

Getting to know
My lonesome self
At end of life...
I wanna cry

Getting to know
This goddamn life
Now far too late...
I won't wake up

Getting to know
Just you and me
We're so lonely...
Eternity

God Is Waiting

And when the sun
Rising for mine
Such sleepy time
I can't now wake
Angels whispering:
God is waiting Now

God's Always

He's leaving now
Footprints in sand
My mind's imprints
God's always there
God's Present

Such jubilation
Life's celebration

Goin' Home

Goin' home
This last night
Such long time
Without bread
Without broads
Without sex
Without name
Still...I'm sane
Still...I'm game
Life's insane

Good Friendless Night

It was a good night
In spite of no friends
No guides along way
Lighting my door's path

Hangover

Wakening
To goddamn
Awful blues...
Stoned on life

Honest Question

If you now speak
What you feel
Will you embrace
Such honesty?

Hungry

Love of
Money
Honey
Sugar
Baby
Hungry
Destroys

I Care

You think
I don't
Give a damn
About you

I Give A Damn!

I Love Today

I know
'bout this
Moment
Because
Yesterday's
So far gone
Today's just
Happening
Tomorrow
Such future
Less sorrow
To borrow
Wonderful
Such great life
Oui, memere
Oui, je t'aime
Aujourd'hui

I'm Dyin'

Are you now
So damn well
Kiddin' me...
Your life's dead?
You're cursin?

I'm dyin'!

In His Lost Shadow

Do you care
If I'm dead...
Your shadow
Following
Your lost son
'til he was
So reborn?

In Stilled Life

He's screaming
At damn me
Wake me up
In stilled life

In The Name Of The Father The Son The Holy Spirit

Nothing's worth
Such damn pain
God wouldn't
Forgive this
Worldly sin

Karma

In gratitude
In solitude
In attitude
Karma's
The same
We blame
For lame
We're dead
Alive...
'til then

Kerouac Won

We were soldiers
Lost in battle
Of goddamn words...
Kerouac won!

Kerouac's Anguish

I wanna cry
And don't know how

Kerouac's Blood

Let me bleed
'til I'm dead...
Then I've lived

Kerouac's Dream Escape

You damn messed up
As football star...
Or didn't you?
Couldn't forgive you

You wrote such
Profound words
Baffled mind
Scattered sound

You were so
Crazy shy
Even in your lie...
Until when you died

Kerouac's Last Call

Such damn last call
For alcohol
My brain's on fire
For such desire
Body can't fathom
The ghostly phantom

Kerouac's Last Vision

No more crying
For lost dying
Eyes can now only see
Other reality

Kerouac's No Phoney

I make
No damn
Shit-faced
Sorry
That would
Make me
Phoney

I so
Damn hate
Phoney

Believe

Kerouac's Pain

Really
Don't like
Liquor...
It's quicker
For the pain

Kerouac's Sorrow

I'll
Now cry
For you

For my
Sorrow

Kerouac's Suffering

I ain't worth
Such God's love
'til I've suffered...
Granted you love

Kerouac's Technique

Writing with speed
Of mastermind
To forget death
Master my life

Kerouac's Thoughts

His such thoughts
In my mind
Daring me
To be free

Killer Self

Run run run
How far did
You damn get
Before you
Discovered
You damn killed
That human
Part of you
Part of me
Just human
Now damn dead

Lack Of Soul

I must lack a soul
'cause I don't give a damn
'bout your rock n roll

Life And Death

Life awakening in bliss of morning
Death resurrecting to the mourning

Life's Hold

Dreams despair
When nightmares
Cometh in
Such repair

Lifespan

Yesterday
Lost today
Just buried
Tomorrow
Will go on
Less sorrow
For morrow

Living Dream

Those that dream...
Nightmares come
Those that live
That damn dream...
Nightmares succumb

Lost In Forever

I'm so lost now
More than ever
In forever

Lost Life

What the goddamn
'bout this lost life
Wakin' to mournin'
Starvin' 'til thirstin'
Dyin' forever
I can't cry no damn more
Refuse to be your whore

Lost...In Life

I now wake
In damn waste
Such distaste
For Mistake

Love's Dead

Love's now dead
Christ no God
In my sight

Maybe Jesus Or Satan

Maybe I was meant
To be innocent
Grown into Christ
Man of the cloth

Maybe I was meant
To be damn devil
Grown into damn sin
Hangin' out with Satan

Maybe I was meant
To be just human
Grown into just love
Disciple of God

Mirror's Reflection

As light beckons
Darkness follows
Mirror's reflection
Casts such damning doubt

Mourning

World's apart
Not forgotten
By begotten

Naturally High

Love's like
Angel
Flying
So high
On God

Nearing The End

As I live now
And fading fast
I see White Light
In damn darkness...
My heart so crushed

No Damned Drugs

I will fly
So damn high
On life's sigh
Never cry

No Life

Such death
In life
Cries out
For more
Not dead...no life

No Mistake About My Mistakes

I sit there
In such crap...
Cold darkness
Light evades...
Darkened soul
Yet... I wake...
No mistake

No Respect

Why they shit on me
When they've buried me?

Non-Poet

Can the non-poet see
Through the eyes of blindness
Light blazing through the skies
And knowing when one dies?

Not Long Enough

Guzzling
The damn
Brandy
Waiting
For fine
Champagne
Happy
Damned New
Year

Now Catch 22

Why tolerate hypocrisy
When you can live in misery?

Now That I'm Dead

I just
Wanna
Hear
Your heart
Beating
Keeping
Just us
Alive
Now that
I'm dead
And you're
Alive

Ode To Kerouac's Beast - Inspired by Susan Williams' Comments About My Kerouac Poems

She was a monster
Goddamn had to be
To put up with me
Couldn't help pounding
The hell out of her
Day in and night out
Goddamn booze and drugs
Cursing all night long
Never any sleep
But she was my love
She was my passion
Cried when I tossed her

In garbage heaven
Lives my typewriter

One God

No gods
Just One
Guides us
Through All

Only...Human

To only cry...
And not shed such
Tears of pain
Tears of joy
Only...human

To only see...
And thus shed light
From such scared blindness
What is great wisdom
Only...human

To only hear...
From sad songs of love
Blissful harmony
With this sacred life
Only...human

Overjoyed

Such depth
To in-depth
Of the soul...
Always cry

Pilgrim

Once a pauper
Lost in diaper
Now a pilgrim
Found in Kingdom

Pinching Won't Wake Me

When I wake
Please touch me
Sight to see
Such glory
Hearing such
Great music
Now touching
Majesty
Please pinch mc
To wake me

Poor Self Esteem

I ain't worth
Such a damn
As to screw
Your life's worth

I'm...human

A Note from the Author

If you enjoyed this book, I would greatly appreciate if you could write a review and publish it at your point of purchase. Your review, regardless of length, will assist other readers in deciding if they'll enjoy my writings.

www.ingramcontent.com/pod-product-compliance
Lightning Source LLC
LaVergne TN
LVHW091117150826
845673LV00002B/863

* 9 7 8 9 3 6 3 5 4 2 7 2 3 *